Capsized

by Dr. Randy Johnson

with contributions by:

Noble Baird
Jared Bruder
Caleb Combs
Carole Combs
Jayson Combs
Jen Combs
Donna Fox
Michael Fox
Danielle Hardenburg
Sue Harrington
Matt Hatton
Josh Lahring
Chuck Lindsay
Jill Osmon
Dani Reynolds
Ryan Story
Ty Woznek

First Edition, June 2016

Published by:
The River Church
8393 E. Holly Rd.
Holly, MI 48442

Scriptures are taken from the Bible,
English Standard Version (ESV)

THE RIVER CHURCH

Printed in the United States of America

CONTENTS

WEEK 4: STORM CHASER

1

STORM WARNING

Pastor Chuck Lindsay | Reach Pastor

"*And when he got into the boat, his disciples followed him. And behold, there arose a great storm on the sea, so that the boat was being swamped by the waves; but he was asleep. And they went and woke him, saying, "Save us, Lord; we are perishing." And he said to them, "Why are you afraid, O you of little faith?" Then he rose and rebuked the winds and the sea, and there was a great calm. And the men marveled, saying, "What sort of man is this, that even winds and sea obey him?"* (Matthew 8:23-27)

"'Follow Me!' he said, 'Follow Me!' Look where that's got us!" – Those are the words I imagine the disciples of Jesus saying in the middle of the Sea of Galilee as the worst storm they had ever seen began to violently throw their boat around.

The entire scene unfolds midway through the eighth chapter of Matthew's Gospel. Jesus has just finished telling each of them to, that is right, you guessed it...*"Follow Me."* To their credit, that is just what they do. They leave behind the world they have known to follow Him into a life they do NOT yet know. Beginning in Matthew 8:23 we read the words, *"And when He got into the boat, His disciples followed Him."* Kudos boys!

Now, I am sure they thought this would be a leisurely glide across a familiar sea. These guys are not rookies; many of them were seasoned fishermen. They had been on this sea hundreds, if not, thousands of times. However, this night would be very different.

In verse 24, the whole scene abruptly changes. ***"And behold, there arose a great storm on the sea."*** Like something out of a movie, a storm, the likes of which they have never seen, cuts through the calm and throws everything into chaos. Sound familiar? Is this how storms seem to come up in your life? Yeah, me too. One minute it is calm, the next is chaos. As the story continues, it becomes clear that these seasoned seamen are totally overwhelmed. The words of verse 24 graphically show this, ***"so that the boat was being swamped by the waves."*** That is a gentle way of saying that the boat is going down and with them in it!

Now, where is Jesus in all of this? Wasn't He in the boat? What was He doing? Was He shouting out instructions? Was He calming everyone down? Was He joining in to keep the boat from capsizing? Nope. None of the above. The last four words of verses 24 tell us simply, ***"but He was asleep."*** Did you read that? He is asleep!

Ok, close your eyes and try to picture what is going on here. The sky is dark, the wind is howling, rain is sideways and pouring down on them as wave after wave brings the boat up and then sends it crashing down. Wave after wave comes in what seems to be an endless succession and the little boat is taking on water. These Navy veterans are powerless to the storm's power. It is too big for them! All their experience and strength has yielded nothing.

There is Jesus, we are told in Mark's Gospel, ***"in the stern, asleep on a pillow."***

Has this described your last week, month, or year? _____

_____

_____

_____

Perhaps it is your marriage, your children, or your health.

_____

_____

_____

A storm, the likes of which you have never known, has suddenly arisen in your life. It is fierce, and it is throwing you. Wave after wave crashes into every area of your little "boat." Waves of fear, worry, and pain. Oh sure, you have your "ups" where you know the Lord is in control, but then like the boat that day, down you go into despair. Side to side from this thought to that. As you read this, you have spent all your energy, and it has not changed a thing. You feel like you are taking on water, and everything inside you says, "you are going to drown, this storm is too big, it will be the end of you." Oh, and Jesus is asleep.

Is it any surprise that once they have exhausted their own resources, they finally turn to Jesus for His help? _____

_____

_____

_____

The story goes on to tell us that the disciples wake Jesus and say this, "save us!" That is not all they say, for Mark's Gospel tells us they despairingly ask Him a question. They ask, ***"Don't you care that we are going to die?"***

Oh, that is the question, isn't it? In the middle of your storm today, the one you are going through as you read this… the question we end up asking is, "Why aren't you helping us? Don't you care? Why are you asleep in my time of need? Why aren't you intervening? Why aren't we hearing anything from you? Don't you care about us?"

Do you ever wonder if God cares? _____
_____
_____
_____

How has someone comforted you with God's love in the past or how have you corrected your own thinking when feeling alone and like no one cares? _____
_____
_____
_____

If the story stopped there, it would be a very sad story indeed. However, it is not where it ends, not by a long shot. You see, there was a purpose in this storm. It was not random happenstance. There is a purpose in your storm. In verse 26 Jesus asks them, *"Why are you afraid, O you of little faith?"* He was essentially saying, "Guys, what are you so worked up over?" That is kind of an odd thing to say to them considering the circumstances, isn't it? It sure seems odd when He says it to you and me in the midst of our storm. However, He has actually put His finger RIGHT ON THE ISSUE; He is saying, "Don't you trust Me?" According to Jesus, it is just simple math, they are afraid = they do not trust Him.

Do you agree that it is a trust issue? _____

_____

_____

_____

Oh sure, they trust Him in certain things just as you do. However, do they trust Him in this life-threatening situation? They just do not know. They do not know if He is in control. They do not know if they are safe. They do not know if He can handle this. They do not know.

Are trust issues also control issues? _____

_____

_____

_____

So that is what this storm is about, and that is what your storm is about.

You see, the disciples ask TWO questions in this story. We have already mentioned the first one, "Don't you care?" the second will come at the end of the story after He puts His hand out and calms the storm with a word (verse 26). That second question? *"Who is this?"* You see, this storm did more than cut through the calm of night, it cut through them. It revealed their weakness. It exposed their hearts and minds. It was masterfully used by the Master to teach them two truths: 1. He does care. 2. He was in control.

In truth, they had no reason to worry, no reason to fear. They were never actually in danger. "How can you say that?" you might ask. Because Jesus said it, *"Why did you fear?"* You see, He said to them, as they got into that boat (something you would not know until you read the other Gospel accounts of this story), *"Let us cross to the other side."* Guess what? They made it to the other side. They did not drown. They were ALWAYS going to make it to the other side. Always.

Jesus knew this, and so He was asleep. However, they did not know they would make it to the other side did they? Yet, Jesus said it, Jesus was with them, and Jesus knew it. It becomes an issue of trust. What about you? You do not know everything that is going to happen, but you do know Him. Do you know that He cares? Do you know that He is with you? Do you know that He is good? That He is able? That He has a plan? If you do not, He is going to prove it to you, through this storm you are in today.

Do you agree God cares? That He is with you? That He is good? That He is able? That He has a plan? _____

_____

_____

_____

Perhaps He seems asleep? He is in control. Perhaps He is silent? He cares. Perhaps He is not leading? He has a plan. Is it ever going to end? He calmed it with a word. Trust Him. Trust Him. Trust Him.

One last thing we cannot miss in this story. In light of all this, we realize something; they could have been resting too. They could have been resting with Jesus. Instead, because they are unsure of Him, they are exhausted, doubting, and filled with debilitating fear! Hebrews 4:9 tells us that *"there remains therefore a rest for the people of God, let us be careful to enter that rest."* This rest, in the midst of a storm, comes from being sure about Jesus, who He is and if He cares.

Therefore, to summarize, this storm had a purpose. Your storm has a purpose. It is to make us sure of Him, who He is and if He cares. These are always our trouble in storms. Who is He really? Is He the all-powerful, all capable God that we have thought Him to be? Can He really be healer? Can he really be Counselor? Can He really be the one who fixes marriages, gives hope, and has a plan etc? The question remains, "Does He really care?" Maybe you have asked, "God I know that you are able, but I don't know if you WANT TO?" "Do you care about my situation? My STORM? DO you SEE what I am going through? Why are you so silent?"

Can you think of a storm from your past that has already proven to have had value? _____

_____

_____

_____

However, it is through storms that we learn such important life anchoring truths... He is with us. He loves us deeply. He is in control. He has a plan. We are safe with Him.

Trust Him. Trust Him. Trust Him.

Jeremia 12:11
2 Cron. 20:12
Phil 4:6-7
Roman 8:28.
1 Thes. 5:16-18

GOD USES STORMS TO TEACH US

Danielle Hardenburg | Nursery & Pre-K Director

O ne touch of a hot stove, a fall from a height and the air knocked from your chest, feeling the sting from a deep cut or a broken bone...

We all resist pain and even run from it. What if we never experienced God's design of physical pain? How would we safeguard our physical bodies? Would it change how our children learn about their world? Some of the physical pain we face teaches us, it can protect us, or even change our point of view. At every stage of life, we have often learned from discomfort and those lessons can be vivid because of the pain that was caused.

The Bible says in Matthew 14:22-24, *"And straightway Jesus constrained his disciples to get into a ship, and to go before him unto the other side, while he sent the multitudes away. And when he had sent the multitudes away, he went up into a mountain apart to pray: and when the evening was come, he was there alone. But the ship was now in the midst of the sea, tossed with waves: for the wind was contrary."*

Why would Jesus constrain or send His disciples to get into a boat and head out into a coming storm? Facing a storm in the night where they were "tossed with waves" and soaked to the bone, I believe the disciples probably wondered where Jesus was and prayed the storm would end so they could make it safely to the other side.

The Bible says in Matthew 14:25-27, *"And in the fourth watch of the night Jesus went unto them, walking on the sea. And when the disciples saw him walking on the sea, they were troubled, saying It is a spirit; and they cried out for fear. But straightway Jesus spake unto them, saying Be of good cheer: it is I; be not afraid."*

Jesus did not simply answer the disciples' prayers and just end the storm they were in. Instead, He met them out in the middle of it, walking on the waves. There is no doubt that He heard them cry out for Him, but instead of changing His friends' circumstances He walked through the storm with them. In the Bible, Jesus says in John 16:33, *"In this world you will have trouble."* It does not say you might or could have trouble; it says you will. However, Jesus also says, *"But take heart! I have overcome the world."* Does that change the view of the struggles you are facing today?

GOD NEVER SAYS "UH-OH."

Danielle Hardenburg | Nursery & Pre-K Director

T he Bible says in Mathew 14:28-31, *"And Peter answered him and said, Lord, if it be thou, bid me come unto thee on the water. And he said, Come. And when Peter was come down out of the ship, he walked on the water, to go to Jesus. But when he saw the wind boisterous, he was afraid; and beginning to sink, he cried, saying, Lord, save me. And immediately Jesus stretched forth his hand, and caught him, and said unto him, O thou of little faith, wherefore didst thou doubt?"*

In the very middle of the mess, Jesus met them and Peter called out for Him. In the midst of a storm Jesus answered, building Peter's faith and reliance upon Him and He said, *"Come."* We are all guaranteed storms, but we are never alone in them. God will see us through our trials, and our suffering produces a reliance on Him. When we are humble and fix our eyes, we can walk (or run) to Jesus and hold His hand to make it through. We ALL have faced trials that caused great **emotional** pain, and when these circumstances are recalled to memory, the pain can be as fresh as it was at the moment we lived it. Anger, hurt, and sadness can rock our lives. These emotional discomforts, and how we deal with them, continuously shape and edify us. However, through all the storms that life is promised to bring us, we can cling to a solid truth. God has a divine purpose in the pain. Our job is to trust Him through the storm and wait to see the spiritual fruit that accompanies it.

God never says, "Uh-Oh."
He is never caught off-guard.
He comes to us in the storm and offers us to walk with Him.

PROCRASTINATION

Dani Reynolds | Graphic Designer

A bout a month ago I was asked to write a devotion on why God uses storms to teach us. As soon as I was asked, I began to panic. The devil was working in me and taunting my thoughts with "I don't know much about the Bible. How am I going to be able to write this? I asked, "Are you sure you want me to write this devotion? I really don't know the Bible that well to be able to write a devotion that someone else may learn from." I was told you will be fine, just ask the other people in your group and bounce ideas off one another you will be able to help each other. I laughed and made a few jokes about how I think someone made a mistake by asking me to write this devotion. I decided to look up the verses that were given to me Matthew 14:22-33 as a reference, but I was not able to make any sense of it. I was clueless on what to write about. I started to get agitated that I did not know what to do. I asked a few folks in my group what we are supposed to write about, and they gave me some examples, but I was not really listening. I really did not want to write the devotion. I did not want to look like I didn't know what I was talking about. So, I decided procrastination was the best option, and I will write the paper later.

Ecclesiastes 11:4 says, ***"Whoever watches the wind will not plant; whoever looks at the clouds will not reap."*** This verse basically means if you wait and do not do what your supposed to do, you will never get it done. That is the story of my life. I tend to procrastinate. I did not realize, until my light bulb came on, that procrastinating only makes things worse. I broke down and gave in and prayed to God that I could finally figure out what I am to write about. I reached out to Him and said, "Please God help me! Show me what I am to write about." Now that my attention is on

19

God, and I am begging Him to help me through my devotional writing journey, I am now able to share why God gives us storms. Storms are to teach us that we need Him. God is the answer. God is the rock in my storm. If I feel like I am ill equipped to handle a project, then I am to go to Him. Ask Him to guide me through the storm and not to rely on myself because when I do that I become vulnerable to what the devil wants me to believe that I am not good enough or that I will fail so why even try. I need to focus on Jesus and stay in the Word so that way I am prepared for the next storm that will come along.

"That, however, is not the way of life you learned" (Ephesians 4:20 NIV). Christ did not teach us to procrastinate. He taught us to do things now. Be always ready to take on the storms of life. If I had been studying in God's Word all along, I would have had the knowledge to have confidently written my devotion and had it turned in on time. *"I can do all this through him who gives me strength"* (Philippians 4:13 NIV). Since I was not prepared for this storm in writing a devotion and having it turned in on time, I failed. God uses storms to teach us that if we are prepared and follow His Word we will succeed. Storms are going to happen whether we are prepared or not. If we allow God to train us on how to handle storms in our life we will not fail. The devil will not get the victory, God will. People are constantly watching especially if you call yourself a Christian. If I were not leading by example, then why would anyone want to get to know Jesus? If I am claiming Jesus is where it is at but I do not use His teachings during a storm, then how am I to show others that God is the almighty protector.

If you find yourself hearing the devil whisper his ugly words, remember what Isaiah 28:16 (NIV) says, *"So this is what the Sovereign Lord says: 'See, I lay a stone in Zion, a tested stone, a precious cornerstone for a sure foundation; the one who relies on it will never be stricken with panic.'"*

TIDAL WAVES

Sue Harrington | Secretary

Definition of Storm: attack, disturbance, warning

Attack: Raid, invade, charge
Disturbance: Turmoil, uprising, disruption
Warning: Threatening, caution, realization

Our sea of life moves along smoothly for the most part and then all of a sudden it seems as if we are blind-sided by the biggest storm or sometimes a tidal wave. Storms are not comfortable, and there are sometimes no warnings about what is to come. It does, however, give us a great opportunity to tune into God and His Word and learn that He IS our best friend. He is the one we CAN count on, rely on, cry out to, and beg Him to not only hold our hand but to carry us when we feel weak. Although it sometimes feels like we will never be able to crawl out of the depths of this stormy sea, we can with the help and promises of God. He is always there waiting for us to call out His name and say, "Lord, I am sinking, and I need you to rescue me."

I then reflect on when God saved Daniel from the lions' den. Can you imagine being thrown into a den like that and having the faith that God would save you from the horrible death that would occur? I know it is hard because we cannot see God or touch Him or believe that we will get through the storm, but His timing is not our timing, His timing is without delay in every circumstance, and it is our job just to keep praying and thanking Him for the outcome and for answered prayer. Romans 8:28 says, *"We are assured and know that (God being a partner in our labor) ALL things work together and are (fitting into a plan) for good to and for those who love God and are called according*

to (His) design and purpose." Isaiah 43:2 says that when we pass through the waters, He is with us, and through the rivers, they will not overwhelm us and when we walk through the fire, we will not be burned or scorched, nor will the flame kindle upon us. We really have to read these promises and trust and believe that what He says is true! In Matthew 8:23-27 Jesus was sleeping in the boat and the storm came and the disciples were so afraid that they were going to drown. They woke Him up saying, "Lord save us." He asked why they were so afraid. He got up and rebuked the winds and waves, and it became completely calm.

So why then do we panic in times of hardship and trials? We are human and weak. We become afraid we are not going to make it, but He is God almighty and strong. The one who created the heavens, the earth, put the sky, stars in place, and spoke light and darkness into existence. He raised Lazarus from the dead, He parted the Red Sea, He took on the sins of the world and died a horrible death and would have done it for just one person. That person is you and me. We need to have more faith and trust in who He is. He is INCREDIBLE! He uses the storms in our lives to teach us to depend on Him. There is a rainbow at the end of it all, and there is a calmness on the horizon when we trust Him, but remember He wants ALL of us, EVERYTHING, not just what we want to give but He requires it ALL! He is in the calming business. So have faith my friends and make Him Lord of your life! He is worthy and He is worth it!

BE STRONG AND COURAGEOUS

Dr. Randy Johnson | Growth Pastor

Transitions in life can be scary. There is an excitement of moving up to high school, going off to college, getting married, starting a new job, having a child, moving for another new job, and eventually retiring, but with the excitement comes a little bit of uneasiness. We do not have full control and "What if." Fear can set in without an apparent foe, and we wonder what if such and such happens.

Moses "celebrates" his 120th birthday. He knows it is time for a new general. God tells Moses it is to be Joshua. Joshua is typically viewed as a man's man kind of hero. However, in Deuteronomy 31:6 Moses tells Joshua, *"Be strong and courageous. Do not fear or be in dread of them, for it is the Lord your God who goes with you. He will not leave you or forsake you."* Moses' first advice is for Moses to *"Be strong and courageous."* Moses warns Joshua that storms will come, and he needs to *"Be strong and courageous."* One would think that the mighty Joshua would only need to be reminded once. Moses repeats himself in Deuteronomy 31:7, 23; Joshua 1: 6, 9, 18 and says in Joshua 1:7, *"Be strong and very courageous."* Moses adds the word "very" for added emphasis. Moses tells Joshua seven times!

Deuteronomy 31:6 implied a warning of future storms, gave the command to hold your ground, and gave the means by which it can be done, *"Do not fear or be in dread of them, for it is the Lord your God who goes with you. He will not leave you or forsake you."* God is with us in the storm. He will not leave us. He will not forsake or abandon us. We do not know exactly when the storm is coming, how it is coming, or even why it is coming. However, all we need to know is God is with us. He has a reason.

He has a plan. He may even have a lesson plan and is waiting to teach us something special.

Psalm 107:28-31 sounds like it is from the Gospels, ***"Then they cried to the Lord in their trouble, and he delivered them from their distress. He made the storm be still, and the waves of the sea were hushed. Then they were glad that the waters were quiet, and he brought them to their desired haven. Let them thank the Lord for his steadfast love, for his wondrous works to the children of man!"***

God cares about us and is with us in our storms. We need to keep our eyes focused on Him at all times.

We do not know what the future holds, but we know Who holds the future.

LONG WAY FROM LAND

Carole Combs | Wife of Lead Pastor Jim Combs

M y dad was listening to the transistor radio (if you do not know what this is, ask your parents or grandparents) because the weather began to look rough outside. All of a sudden he told all of our family that we were going into the basement to take shelter from the storm. As a little girl, I was not sure that it was much safer in our spider-ridden dirt Michigan basement. My dad knew this was a safer place. Sometimes the Lord takes us places we do not want to go to keep us safe from the real storms of life.

In Matthew 14:24, it says that the boat by this time was a long way from the land beaten by the waves, for the wind was against them. You may be feeling right now that your boat is sinking. It is being beaten by the waves of this world, and you feel like the only thing you are doing is bailing water. The verse goes on to say that the wind was against them. You may also feel that everyone around you is against you. The disciples in the boat thought that life was over for them that night. Here is the best part of this account.

Jesus said, *"Take heart, it is I. Do not be afraid."* Jesus knew they were in the storm, and he was with them. The same is true today. The Lord knows the storms you are in. He is with you. *"Be strong and courageous. Do not fear or be in dread of them, for it is the Lord your God who goes with you. He will NOT leave you or forsake you"* (Deuteronomy 31:6).

Sometimes we cannot prevent the storms that we go through. Often there are warning signs. My dad heeded the warning that day to protect his family. Lighthouses were placed strategically to prevent the ships from crashing against the rocks. Dash lights in our vehicles are meant to warn us of a vehicle problem (or annoy us, for those who ignore them. I am not naming any names). On a daily basis, there are many warnings to keep us safe.

How do I stop my soul from crashing against the rocks? How do I know if this is what I am supposed to do or where I am supposed to go? How can I feel safe from the storms of life? The Word of God not only will warn you of danger, but it will also teach you, lead you, and comfort you. *__For the word of God is living and active...__* (Hebrews 4:12).

Even if you are a long way from land (God), He is waiting for you.

2

STORM SHELTER

Pastor Caleb Combs | Gathering Pastor

Whe I think of the word shelter, one idea comes to mind, Survivor. My wife and I watch this show pretty religiously (ok, get the mocking out of the way). We love to sit down and watch the show together, guessing who will win the ultimate prize and be the sole survivor. However, on the first day of getting to the island or place they will be deserted for the next 40 days unless voted off earlier, they must begin to work together to build a shelter. Over the years, we have seen some poorly built shelters. My personal favorite is "Joe builder guy" that tells everyone he knows how to build the perfect shelter and next thing you know the shelter cannot hold a drop of rain. Ok, rant over making fun of the poor shelters made on survivor. However, if you have ever seen the show, there is usually a stretch during their time on the island when the weather turns bad. The wind and water crash onto their rickety shelter and the survivors huddle underneath palm leaves and other things they have scavenged to build their shelter. The harder the storm, the worse the shelter looks, and you begin to see cracks and holes in it.

Now put this into perspective into storms that happen in our lives. Man, do we think we know how to handle storms and build shelters on our own. We think to ourselves, "Don't worry, I can handle the intensity of this storm all on my own!" However, just like clockwork our shelters leak with rain and crumble under the wind of this world. Let's look at a story in Matthew 8 where we see who and where we can find shelter.

"And when he got into the boat, his disciples followed him. 24 And behold, there arose a great storm on the sea, so that the boat was being swamped by the waves; but he was asleep. 25 And they went and woke him, saying, 'Save us, Lord; we are perishing.' 26 And he said to them, 'Why are you afraid, O you of little faith?' Then he rose and rebuked the winds and the sea, and there was a great calm. 27 And the men marveled, saying, 'What sort of man is this, that even winds and sea obey him?'" (Matthew 8:23-27)

How did the disciples find themselves in the storm and why were they there? _____
_____
_____
_____

"And when He got into the boat, His disciples followed Him. And behold, there arose a great storm on the sea, so that the boat was being swamped by the waves; but he was asleep."

Have you felt like you have been following God and doing everything right and yet the storms still come and rattle your life? How was your response to God? _____
_____
_____
_____
_____

Verse 24 is a description of many of our situations; it says the waves COVERED the boat. Have you felt covered by the storms on this life and felt there is no way out? _____

_____

_____

_____

_____

The disciples panicked and ran to Jesus, who was asleep in the boat.

Do you ever wonder how and why Jesus was asleep? _____

_____

_____

_____

_____

"The only way God can show us He is in control is to put us in situations where we cannot control." Pastor Steven Furtick

Do you agree with this quote? _____

_____

_____

_____

"And they went and woke him, saying, 'Save us, Lord; we are perishing.' And he said to them, 'Why are you afraid...'"

I ask you the same question today, "Why are you afraid?"

_____

_____

_____

_____

The disciples found themselves in a circumstance they could not control. What is weird about this is that four of them were experienced fisherman. I think we forget this fact when reading this story. Peter, Andrew, James, and John has grown up fishing the Sea of Galilee and surely had experienced storms before, but in this storm their past experiences and skills were not good enough. Everything was out of their control. They had to rely on the power of Jesus to get them out of it.

"Jesus responded to them, 'O you of little faith?'"

Have you had a time in your life when you had little faith?

_____

_____

_____

_____

How did you feel and how did you respond to the storm?

_____

_____

_____

_____

Verse 26 tells us, **"He Rose."** Why do you think He rose before He performed the miracle? _____

_____

_____

_____

Jesus did not have to move to stop the storm, he could have continued to lay on His pillow, get His zzzz's on, and stop the storm, but He chose to rise and show these men His ultimate power. Jesus was making a clear statement to the men that no matter what circumstance or situation they find themselves in, Jesus can rise above anything.

We then have the opportunity to see Jesus rebuke the wind and the waves and perform an incredible miracle. As soon as He spoke to the wind and waves, they went calm. The power of Jesus is endless. Ok that may not seem like it has a ton to do with the study guide, but knowing Jesus' power is endless. It is a comforting feeling. The disciples marveled at Jesus and could not totally comprehend who this "man" was. We like having everything under our control, but it is then limited because we are limited. Letting God have full control means there is no limit to His blessing.

"And the men marveled, saying, 'What sort of man is this, that even winds and sea obey him?'"

The men stood amazed at who Jesus was, and they would need to cling to Jesus more as time went on. Jesus took them onto the boat to test their faith and build in them a need for Him.

James 1:2-3 says, *"Count it all joy, my brothers, when you meet trials of various kinds, for you know that the testing of your faith produces steadfastness."* Passing quizzes makes us better prepared for tests.

How has your faith been tested? _____

_____

_____

_____

_____

How can you count it joyful when the storms of life hit?

_____

_____

_____

_____

The disciples' faith was tested in the storm, and they reacted poorly. They did not trust in Jesus that He was in control and all powerful. They feared for their lives, and their faith did not hold. These 12 men needed to come to the realization that they could not rely on their experiences or skills to get through the storm, but they needed to run to Jesus in the storm, and He would be their shelter and protection. Jesus knew these men's faith would be tested many times in the near future, and this storm would shape and strengthen their faith in Him. Many of them were mocked, beaten, and brutally killed because their faith became steadfast in Jesus. God rose up and stood beside them.

How have you used your own skills to try to fight through a storm?

_____

_____

_____

_____

How has it worked for you? _____

_____

_____

_____

How can you better practically "wake up" Jesus in the storms of your life? _____

_____

_____

We discussed the idea of shelters and what and where we can find them. The disciples learned one big thing in their story that no matter what their skill level was and what they knew, they had to rely on the power of Jesus and He is the shelter and relief from the storm. The term shelter means a place of protection or reprieve. We know that in this life we will experience storms, but we know that no matter the circumstance we can hide in the shelter of Jesus Christ. He is our shelter, and we need to build our lives on Him. We need to not be like the guy on survivor that "knows" how to build a shelter that ultimately will crumble under the pressure of the storm. Jesus the ultimate shelter will never crumble and has no cracks. We can hide in Him.

I Peter 5:6-7 says, ***"Humble yourselves, therefore, under the mighty hand of God so that at the proper time he may exalt you, casting all your anxieties on him, because he cares for you."***

As we persevere in trials and humble ourselves by letting go of the reins of life, God will rise and take control. Listen, He is saying, "I have everything under control."

FOR YOUR GLORY AND FOR ME

Pastor Ryan Story | Student Pastor

One of the most beautiful sights in the world is when you are on a road trip and it is a bright, magnificent day, and you see storm clouds on the horizon. Something about seeing the dark heavy clouds in the distance while the sun is still on your shoulders makes for some fun internal dialogue. There becomes a wired sense of panic and excitement that starts to boil up in us. Then we start going though the storm; let us all be honest sometimes you have started driving through a rain storm, and you start white knuckling your steering wheel while others are as calm as can be. Many times while going through a storm, both metaphorically and literally, I tend only to think of myself. Often while going through a storm, I catch myself thinking, "It is not the storm I am worried about it is the morons around me that I am worried about."

If you spend some time reading Matthew 8:23-27, you will see a very popular story involving Jesus and His disciples. The straightforward application and meaning of the story is to show Jesus' authority, power, and glory over all things. However, when we dig a little bit more in the story, we can see that Jesus is teaching more than just that. While I was reading Matthew 8, a puzzling thought came to my mind. If Jesus knows all things (one of the perks of being omniscient), why would He choose to take a boat to get to Gadarenes? Every sane person who has ever been boating knows that you do not stay on the lake during a storm! Why would Jesus take the risk? Did He just want to prove a point? Was this just an amazing teaching point and He needed water and lightning to get His point across? Did He just want to scare a bunch of fishermen? I could be off, but I had a thought about why He might have wanted to go on a boat hours before a storm blew in.

During that storm, Jesus would have known that 2000 years after it happened that we would be reading it today. He knew I would be writing about it; He knew you would be reading about it. When the storm was at its peak, He knew that Peter, John, Judas, and the others would be teaching us all a lesson. That is a cool thought to ponder. Jesus chose to take them through the storm for His glory, and He chose to take them through the storm for me. At the time Jesus did not have to look at Peter and say, "Hey, dude, I know you are freaking out right now, but there will be a church in Michigan that is going to learn a lot from this moment." The storm that the disciples were going through was used to teach them a lesson, but it was also used to teach us one. Take a second to think about that, the storm you are going through is there to teach you, but also God is using it to teach others.

That idea "it is not the storm I am worried about it is the morons around me that I am worried about" that plagues my mind during storms, came crumbling down while reading this. We go through storms for God's glory and to help others grow closer to Jesus. Storms of life can be devastating. From death all the way to a simple fender bender, they are all storms. Take a moment to think about who is watching your walk with God. Take a moment today and ask yourself if you are ready to let Jesus use your storm to help another person.

IT LOOKS LIKE RAIN

Pastor Ryan Story | Student Pastor

W hen I was a kid, the best place to be on a Friday night was Caesar Land. If you have no idea what Caesar Land was, and you are my age, then you had a very lame childhood. If you are older than I am, you did not have children. Caesar Land was located on Dixie Highway, and it was the place to be. They had a giant play structure, pizza, and the most important thing arcade games. I would spend hours up there playing Street Fighter 2, X-Men, and pinball machines. There is something about a good pinball machine that just brings a smile to my face. Many of the pinball games were great, but my favorite was one called "Whirlwind." Now I wish I could explain how this pinball machine was technologically superior to the others, but I cannot. I wish I could say that this game was my favorite because of the way it was laid out, but I could not. The only reason I was drawn to this game was one single reason when you pulled back the plunger to launch the ball it would say, "It looks like rain." I have no idea why, but Whirlwind and the phrase "it looks like rain" would always grab my attention.

If you have ever been outside in the summer, at some point you have had to see a storm roll in. I can think of many times when I was a kid and my friends and I were playing hockey or swimming we would see a storm rolling in. We would stop playing outside and move the action inside. In our walks with God, have you ever seen a storm rolling in and you did nothing to help your situation. When we see a storm coming in, we have to take action immediately. I know there are times in my life where I know there is a conflict brewing with my wife, and I just sit back and wait for it to hit. I do not advise this, but there are times I know the issue, I know how to resolve the issue, but for some odd reason I just sit back and do nothing as the storm starts in my marriage. I have learned that when I see storm clouds forming, it is best that I avoid the storm or ask Jesus how I am going to get through it. Marriage is just one example of this, but take some time and think, when it looks like rain, are you trying to figure out how to avoid the downpour? 1 Peter 5:8 says, ***"Be watchful. Your adversary the devil prowls around like a roaring lion, seeking someone to devour."*** When we see the clouds rolling in, the devil is lying in wait ready to pick us off. When those clouds are rolling in, do you change your behavior? When you see a storm on the horizon in your life, what do you go and grab, an umbrella or a lightning rod?

When it looks like rain, we all must prepare for the storm. Sometimes that means going inside, sometimes that means barring up windows, but we all must do something when a storm comes rolling in. Next time you start seeing a storm of life, take a moment and figure out how you are going to prepare for it. The lazy idea of "let go and let God" is not the soundest advice. Keep your eyes fixed on Jesus, and next time you find yourself in the beginning parts of a storm, find comfort knowing Jesus will be your guide through it.

STORMS MAKE FOR GOOD SLEEPING WEATHER

Michael Fox | Production Director

Throughout our lives, there will be great storms that will rock our ship. It will also come in many forms and at unexpected times. Some of these storms may be small, while others feel as though they are threatening to rip our lives apart down to the very foundation. Sometimes it will be you alone in the storm or you and your spouse or children or family.

As a young believer, and even now, I often drift to thinking that because I know Jesus, there will be no storms. In Matthew 8, we read about a great storm, where the disciples were in fear for their lives. I think back to the storms in my life. When I was a teenager I had my first car accident, and I remember being afraid. When we were expecting our son, my wife had some complications, and I remember being afraid. My son recently had breathing problems during the night, and I remember being afraid. Through these trials, I often wonder if Jesus is "sleeping."

I heard a statement the other day; "The teacher is always silent during a test." During these trials, it is often easy for us to feel alone and feel like we have to face the storm head on with no one to help. The idea of storms and trials in life always reminds me of the book of Job. God gives everything that Job has to the Devil - his land, his money, and even his health. The only stipulation that God gives the Devil is that he cannot kill Job. Throughout the book of Job, the trials that Job is put through become more and more brutal. Everybody in Job's life is telling him to curse God and die because dying would be better than what he was going through. However, Job holds fast, and he stands firm on what he believes. God says enough is enough and blesses Job beyond his wildest dreams.

What I have found is key to hold onto, and often is not our first reaction during a storm, is that Jesus is right there by our side. He does not always remove the storm, but there is a sweet relief in knowing He will help us through the storm. Jesus calls us to believe and to have faith. He promises to deliver us in Psalm 50:15, *"And call upon me in the day of trouble; I will deliver you, and you shall glorify me,"* ultimately to glorify Him.

Matthew 8:23-27 says, *"And when he got into the boat, his disciples followed him. And behold, there arose a great storm on the sea, so that the boat was being swamped by the waves; but he was asleep. And they went and woke him, saying, 'Save us, Lord; we are perishing.' And he said to them, 'Why are you afraid, O you of little faith?' Then he rose and rebuked the winds and the sea, and there was a great calm. And the men marveled, saying, 'What sort of man is this, that even winds and sea obey him?'"*

Jesus shows us a perfect example to follow in Matthew 8. While the storm was raging, Jesus was sleeping. He had full trust in His Father God that He would protect Him and deliver Him, so that He was able to sleep through the storm. This ultimately shows where our faith should be, fully in Jesus.

WE ALWAYS NEED GOD

Josh Lahring | Production Director

W hen I was young, I was terrified of thunderstorms. Anytime there was a storm at night I would run to my parents' room and sleep on the floor. Now while I was not physically any safer in that room than my own room, there was comfort in being with my parents who were not afraid.

To me, that was my shelter. Being by my parents' side no matter how big or small the storm was. As I got older, I was not afraid of the small stuff because I knew I would be fine. I knew how strong a house was, I knew not to be by the windows if it was windy, I knew that if I needed to, I could run to the basement and probably be fine. I could pretty much take care of myself without needing any help.

It is funny how this is the same way we treat our storms in life. Oh, this one is not so bad, I can handle it; I am strong enough to get through it. Then when it is too much to handle, we finally go to our shelter.

Psalm 46:1-3 says, ***"God is our shelter and strength, always ready to help in times of trouble. Therefore we will not fear though the earth gives way, though the mountains be moved into the heart of the sea, though its waters roar and foam, though the mountains tremble at its swelling."***

How many times are we facing storms in life and we never think to run to our shelter because we think we are fine on our own? We try to endure through it; we think we are strong enough only to find ourselves left wrecked by the storm. We have an amazing God always ready to help us in times of trouble, but we do not go there until we think we need it. In every storm we face in life, big or small, we should run to the One who is in command of the storm we are in.

We can take great comfort in knowing that God is our Shelter.

CONTEXT

Noble Baird | Guest Services Director

I t is funny to me how easily we can forget about the true power of God. We will face illnesses, job loss, relational struggles, financial uncertainties (you fill in the blank), and we will see these problems as almost impossible to overcome. Believe me, I have been here many times myself and have struggled with putting these earthly problems at the center of my life. However, it was also during these times when I realized just how much bigger God is. I know you have heard the classic Christian saying for hard times, "Don't worry, God will take care of it all, Jeremiah 29:11." Now, know my heart when I say this, there is great comfort in that passage if you understand the context. Likewise, we can lose the "context" of our faith at times and forget how BIG our God really is.

In Matthew 8:23-27, Jesus and the disciples are out on a boat when a massive storm comes in. So, naturally, they all freak out and cry to Jesus to save them and calm the storm for the fear of dying in it. Once Jesus comes and calms the storm He says in verse 26, *"Why are you afraid, O you of little faith?"* You see, for those few minutes, the disciples had this storm in the center of their lives. All they could think about was the fact that a storm was raging, and there was no way they were going to live. Jesus saved them, and no harm came to them at all.

"O you of little faith" - If we go back to Jeremiah 29:11 and look at the verse right before it, we can then understand the true reality of verse 11. In verse 10, it reads, *"For thus says the Lord: When seventy years are completed for Babylon, I will visit you, and I will fulfill to you my promise and bring you back to this place."* While verse 11 is true, it took 70 years for

47

that promise to be fulfilled. In our lives, we must never forget the background information of our faith, the foundation of it all, Jesus. If we allow the struggles and hardships we face to take center stage in our lives and place Jesus aside, we are going to be rocked by the storm. However, if we take shelter in Christ while the storm rages around us, then we will see His beautiful plan unfold in our lives. So, as you face the various storms in life, remember Who you need to take shelter in; instead of taking shelter in the storm.

YOUR LOVE NEVER FAILS

Noble Baird | Guest Services Director

I have had the privilege of playing drums for the past eight years of my life. To this day, I still do not understand how or why it happened, but it is truly one of the greatest gifts God has ever blessed me with. During this time, I have played with many different musicians in various venues that I never imagined I would have the privilege of playing in. As time has passed, there are those certain songs that I have played that I keep coming back to and could play over and over again. One of my top five favorites is, "Your Love Never Fails" by Jesus Culture. Not only do I love the catchy intro beat, but also I especially love the lyrics of this song.

As we continue this week's discussion about God being our shelter, I could not help but think about the lyrics in this song. I will be honest; they have brought me peace in some of the worst times of my life. One of the lines in the song goes like this, "And when the oceans rage, I don't have to be afraid, because I know that You love me, Your love never fails." When the disciples were facing the raging storm on the boat, they were afraid. If we are all honest, we have all had plenty of moments in this life where we were afraid. Maybe we were afraid of death, the future, the past, the "what ifs"; whatever it may be, we can lose sight. We lose sight of the One who is standing there by our side, calming the storm before we even see Him doing it.

As you continue throughout this week and month, I challenge you to listen to this song. As you do, really listen to the lyrics, maybe even print them off and read them through. At the end of the day, after all the storms and struggles I have faced, one thing that I have always found constant and never failing is His love. The same is true for you. His love for us will never fail, never end, never hide, and never get lost in the storm. Take shelter in His never failing love.

3

STORM DAMAGE

Pastor Jayson Combs | Family Pastor

I was the guy who was always excited to hear the tornado sirens. I was the guy who always wanted to see a tornado. One day, however, that all changed. My wife and I were attending an outdoor graduation party, one of a current youth group member. As we were eating our food and chatting with others, we all noticed a storm approaching across the southern sky. We quickly finished our meal and decided to head for shelter in our car that happened to be parked a block away in a church parking lot. I vividly remember the wall of rain moving toward us as we picked up the pace to our car. Right before we reached the car, the rain hit hard. Then the wind whipped around, as I had never seen before. In the blink of an eye, a sheet of metal blew off the top the church building, narrowly missing my wife, and slamming into our car. One thought ran through my head; we need to get home, fast! We pulled out of the parking lot watching the traffic lights swing furiously. We turned onto our street, but two trees fell across the road in front of us, causing a power line to explode. We turned the car around to try to find another way home, but every road we chose had an uprooted tree blocking the way. We did manage to make it home safely that day, but the events of that day challenged the way I used to view a storm. I now realize how small, helpless, and powerless I am when it comes to fighting Mother Nature. As a result, I have more respect and appreciation for the power of any given storm.

Do you have a storm story? _____

_____

_____

_____

As a follower of Christ, storms happen. Difficulties, stress, death, and pain, it all happens. So how do we deal with the storms?

_____

_____

_____

1 Peter 4:12-16 says, *"Beloved, do not be surprised at the fiery trial when it comes upon you to test you, as though something strange were happening to you. 13 But rejoice insofar as you share Christ's sufferings, that you may also rejoice and be glad when his glory is revealed. 14 If you are insulted for the name of Christ, you are blessed, because the Spirit of glory and of God rests upon you. 15 But let none of you suffer as a murderer or a thief or an evildoer or as a meddler. 16 Yet if anyone suffers as a Christian, let him not be ashamed, but let him glorify God in that name."*

God clearly (and repeatedly) says that we will have trials in our life. Why do we "Christians" question God while facing the storms of life? _____

_____

_____

_____

Will God always take away the storms in our life? As you consider this question, read Paul's response in 2 Corinthians 12: 9-10 *("But he said to me, 'My grace is sufficient for you, for my power is made perfect in weakness." Therefore I will boast all the more gladly of my weaknesses, so that the power of Christ may rest upon me. For the sake of Christ, then, I am content with weaknesses, insults, hardships, persecutions, and calamities. For when I am weak, then I am strong.")*

_____

_____

_____

_____

What was Peter's struggle in the storm of Matthew 14: 30-31 *("But when he saw the wind, he was afraid, and beginning to sink he cried out, 'Lord, save me.' Jesus immediately reached out his hand and took hold of him, saying to him, 'O you of little faith, why did you doubt?'")*? _____

_____

_____

_____

_____

For me, I often relate to Peter. In the storm, I begin to focus on the wind and not on my Savior. Have you had storms in your life where the wind took your focus off God? _____

_____

_____

_____

What types of storms did Jesus face while He was here on the earth?

He was _____ . Matthew 4:2-3

He had _____ his head. Matthew 8:20

When Jesus heard Lazarus was dead he didn't just heal him, he walked approximately 20 miles.

Peter, his close friend _____ him. Luke 22:54-62

The Disciples _____ over who was better. Mark 9:46

Judas who walked with Jesus _____ Him. John 13:21

Daniel 3: *"King Nebuchadnezzar made an image of gold, whose height was sixty cubits and its breadth six cubits. He set it up on the plain of Dura, in the province of Babylon. 2 Then King Nebuchadnezzar sent to gather the satraps, the prefects, and the governors, the counselors, the treasurers, the justices, the magistrates, and all the officials of the provinces to come to the dedication of the image that King Nebuchadnezzar had set up. 3 Then the satraps, the prefects, and the governors, the counselors, the treasurers, the justices, the magistrates, and all the officials of the provinces gathered for the dedication of the image that King Nebuchadnezzar had set up. And they stood before the image that Nebuchadnezzar had set up. 4 And the herald proclaimed aloud, "You are commanded, O peoples, nations, and languages, 5 that when you hear the sound of the horn, pipe, lyre, trigon, harp, bagpipe, and every kind of music, you are to fall down and worship the golden image that King Nebuchadnezzar has set up. 6 And whoever does not fall down and worship shall immediately be cast into a burning fiery furnace." 7 Therefore, as soon as all the peoples heard the sound of the horn, pipe, lyre, trigon, harp, bagpipe, and every kind of music, all the peoples, nations, and languages fell down and worshiped the golden image that King Nebuchadnezzar had set up.*

8 Therefore at that time certain Chaldeans came forward and maliciously accused the Jews. 9 They declared to King Nebuchadnezzar, "O king, live forever! 10 You, O king, have made a decree, that every man who hears the sound of the horn, pipe, lyre, trigon, harp, bagpipe, and every kind of music, shall fall down and worship the golden image. 11 And whoever does not fall down and worship shall be cast into a burning fiery furnace. 12 There are certain Jews whom you have appointed over the affairs of the province of Babylon: Shadrach, Meshach, and Abednego. These men, O king, pay no attention to you; they do not serve your gods or worship the golden image that you have set up."

13 Then Nebuchadnezzar in furious rage commanded that Shadrach, Meshach, and Abednego be brought. So they brought these men before the king. 14 Nebuchadnezzar answered and said to them, "Is it true, O Shadrach, Meshach, and Abednego, that you do not serve my gods or worship the golden image that I have set up? 15 Now if you are ready when you hear the sound of the horn, pipe, lyre, trigon, harp, bagpipe, and every kind of music, to fall down and worship the image that I have made, well and good. But if you do not worship, you shall immediately be cast into a burning fiery furnace. And who is the god who will deliver you out of my hands?"

16 Shadrach, Meshach, and Abednego answered and said to the king, "O Nebuchadnezzar, we have no need to answer you in this matter. 17 If this be so, our God whom we serve is able to deliver us from the burning fiery furnace, and he will deliver us out of your hand, O king. 18 But if not, be it known to you, O king, that we will not serve your gods or worship the golden image that you have set up."

19 Then Nebuchadnezzar was filled with fury, and the expression of his face was changed against Shadrach, Meshach, and Abednego. He ordered the furnace heated seven times more than it was usually heated. 20 And he ordered some of the mighty men of his army to bind Shadrach, Meshach, and Abednego, and to cast them into the burning fiery furnace. 21 Then these men were bound in their cloaks, their tunics, their hats, and their other garments, and they were thrown into the burning fiery furnace. 22 Because the king's order was urgent and the furnace overheated, the flame of the fire killed those men who took up Shadrach, Meshach, and Abednego. 23 And these three men, Shadrach, Meshach, and Abednego, fell bound into the burning fiery furnace.

24 Then King Nebuchadnezzar was astonished and rose up in haste. He declared to his counselors, "Did we not cast three men bound into the fire?" They answered and said to the king, "True, O king." 25 He answered and said, "But I see four men unbound, walking in the midst of the fire, and they are not hurt; and the appearance of the fourth is like a son of the gods."

26 Then Nebuchadnezzar came near to the door of the burning fiery furnace; he declared, "Shadrach, Meshach, and Abednego, servants of the Most High God, come out, and come here!" Then Shadrach, Meshach, and Abednego came out from the fire. 27 And the satraps, the prefects, the governors, and the king's counselors gathered together and saw that the fire had not had any power over the bodies of those men. The hair of their heads was not singed, their cloaks were not harmed, and no smell of fire had come upon them. 28 Nebuchadnezzar answered and said, "Blessed be the God of Shadrach, Meshach, and Abednego, who has sent his angel and delivered his servants, who trusted in him, and set aside the king's command, and yielded up their bodies rather than serve and worship any god except their own God. 29 Therefore I make a decree: Any people, nation, or language that speaks anything against the God of Shadrach, Meshach, and Abednego shall be torn limb from limb, and their houses laid in ruins, for there is no other god who is able to rescue in this way." 30 Then the king promoted Shadrach, Meshach, and Abednego in the province of Babylon."

What type of storm were Shadrach, Meshach, and Abednego facing? _____

_____

_____

_____

What type of peer pressure do you think they were facing?

_____

_____

_____

Look again at Daniel 3:16-18.

How did they respond to the storm? _____

_____

_____

_____

_____

Did they have a lack of faith because they did not fully believe God would rescue them? _____

_____

_____

_____

Years ago, I taught on the story in Daniel chapter three. I planned to use a large metal garbage bin as a visual aid during the lesson. As I presented to high school students, I went all 'WWE' on the garbage bin and dented it all up. After I finished having my fun with the garbage bin, I related the banged up bin to our lives. The garbage bin represented how storms would damage and dent up their lives. Shadrach, Meshach, and Abednego were also in the midst of a storm. They were facing death as a result of not worshipping the idols set up by King Nebuchadnezzar. Look at their response to the king in the scripture again.

"17 If this be so, our God whom we serve is able to deliver us out of your hand, O king. 18 But if not, be it known to you, O king, that we will not serve your gods..."

Verse 18 proves to be an incredibly powerful verse. They told the king that if God did not deliver them how they thought He should, they still would not serve King Nebuchadnezzar. Shadrach Meshach, and Abednego were B.I.N Christians, "But If Not" Christians. They would not give up. In the midst of trouble and pain, the storm was not going to destroy their testimony or faith in God, even if God did not intervene as they thought God should intervene.

Do you ever struggle with being a "But If Not" Christian? If so, how? _____

_____

_____

_____

Why do you think God would allow his followers to be in storms?

_____

_____

_____

Have you had a storm in your life that brought you closer to God?

_____

_____

_____

THERE IS ALWAYS AN ESCAPE

Jared Bruder | Growth Intern

I n life we experience storms. Some storms are out of our control, and others are a direct result of our actions. One storm that hits us in life is a storm called temptation. This storm can come out of nowhere and hits us in ways that seem like they may break us. In the Bible, Joseph experienced a storm of temptation. This storm came to Joseph while he was a slave in Potiphar's house. This account is recorded in Genesis 39:7-8a that says, *"And after a time his master's wife cast her eyes on Joseph and said, 'Lie with me.' But he refused."* This temptation did not stop there for Joseph. We see in Genesis 39:10 that Potiphar's wife came to Joseph daily, and Joseph continued to refuse. Then the storm intensified in Genesis 39:12 which says, *"She caught him by his garment, saying, Lie with me."* At this point, Joseph looked for a way to escape from this temptation, and he found it. The Bible tells us in the last part of Genesis 39:12, *"He left his garment in her hand and fled and got out of the house."* Joseph found a way of escape for the storm of temptation, and this storm did not break him.

One thing guaranteed in the Christian life is that there will be storms of temptation. Just like Joseph, we must find a way to escape. We are promised in I Corinthians 10:13, *"No temptation has overtaken you that is not common to man. God is faithful, and he will not let you be tempted beyond your ability, but with the temptation he will also provide the way of escape, that you may be able to endure it."* We have been promised that there will be a way of escape. When we find ourselves going through a storm of temptation, we must look for the escape because we know there will be one.

In this life, God does not want us to fail. That is why He has promised with temptation that there will be a way of escape. When you find yourself in temptation and you feel there is no way out, do not lose hope. For God will always provide a way of escape. Look for and find the way of escape and you can endure and have victory over the storms of temptation.

OUT OF MY CONTROL

Jared Bruder | Growth Intern

There are stages in our life that we face hard times. Hard times come and go and for that reason, we call them storms as an illustration. I faced a large storm in my life not all that long ago. I was returning to school for my sixth year of Bible College. After making the one thousand mile drive down to school, I found out just hours after arriving I would not be able to continue my education, and I would have to return home. I had to turn around and make the one thousand mile drive back home. I was entering a world of unknowns. Where would I work? How will I finish my education? What is going to happen? All of my plans for my life seemed to come crashing down. I was a mess. I was stressed out and depressed. I did not know what I was going to do. This storm hit me so hard; I felt I would never get out of it.

I felt like this storm was going to destroy me but then I came across Luke 12:22-26, *"And he said to his disciples, Therefore I tell you, do not be anxious about your life, what you will eat, nor about your body, what you will put on. For life is more than food, and the body more than clothing. Consider the ravens: they neither sow nor reap, they have neither storehouse nor barn, and yet God feeds them. Of how much more value are you than the birds! And which of you by being anxious can add a single hour to his span of life? If then you are not able to do as small a thing as that, why are you anxious about the rest?"* I was reminded that God is in control and that God will take care of me. I began to trust God and ask God for strength to get through this storm that seemed to have no end.

God is faithful, and He brought me through that storm. It was through this storm that at the time I did not understand why it happened but looking back it all makes sense. It was because of this storm that I found The River Church. If it had not been for that storm in my life I would not have the opportunity to reach out to bikers in Flint, I would not have the opportunity to reach out to inmates in prison, and I would not have the opportunity to write and share my story with you. I know from experience that whatever storm you are going through God will bring you through. Trust God and do not lose hope. The storm you are going through will come to an end.

JONAH AND THE EFFECTS OF SIN

Matt Hatton | Student Ministries Director

When I was in high school, I loved taking hands-on science, technology, and physics classes. I enjoyed these classes because they were an easy-A, most of the time, and because we had the opportunities to do many projects that involved building things. One of those projects that I managed to do six times in the span of four years was the infamous "Rube Goldberg" Project. The aim of these projects was to build something where energy would be transferred from one thing to another eventually causing something grand to happen. One push of a domino would have an effect on mousetraps, toy cars, wheels, pulleys, levers, and other random apparatuses that would somehow make their way to turning on a light, making a sound, squeezing toothpaste on a toothbrush, or even starting a car! One small thing had a large effect on many others.

Sin can be like those Rube Goldberg machines. The only difference is that we do not realize how large and detrimental of an impact sin makes not only in our lives but also in the lives of many others. In the book of Jonah chapter 1 we see that Jonah did not realize this either. God commanded Jonah to go to Nineveh and to preach against their wickedness; however, Jonah felt like he would rather do his own thing and not do what God had commanded him to do (That is called sin by the way). As Jonah continued to run from the Lord, as he dove deeper and deeper into disobedience, we begin to see the effects.

"But the Lord hurled a great wind upon the sea, and there was a mighty tempest on the sea, so that the ship threatened to break up. Then the mariners were afraid and each cried out to his own god. And they hurled the cargo that was in the ship into the sea to lighten it for them" (Jonah 1:4-5).

"And they said to one another, 'Come, let us cast lots, that we may know on whose account this evil has come upon us.' So they cast lots, and the lot fell on Jonah" (Jonah 1:7).

"Then they said to him, 'What shall we do to you, that the sea may quiet down for us?' For the sea grew more and more tempestuous. He said to them, 'Pick me up and hurl me into the sea; then the sea will quiet down for you, <u>for I know it is because of me that this great tempest has come upon you</u>'" (Jonah 1:11-12).

The consequences of sin are unmistakable. Sin brings destruction! Sin makes us deserving of an eternal destruction, but it also causes damage that is immediate. We will often face the repercussions for our sin right here and right now. Jonah saw some immediate effects of his sin that made his life pretty rough for a short while. We also see that Jonah was not the only one that faced the storm caused by his sin. There were many others that were affected by it! Everyone else on the boat thought they were going to die all because of the sin of one man! Our sin has immediate consequences in our lives and the lives of others. Have you seen the immediate damage cause by your sin or others? Has your sin affected others? Have you been affected by the sin of others?

DAVID'S DEMISE AND THE DEPTH OF SIN'S DAMAGE

Matt Hatton | Student Ministries Director

Yesterday God showed us in His Word that there are, without a doubt, immediate consequences of our sin. Sometimes they are small and sometimes they are compared with being near to death in the middle of a raging storm. Whatever they may look like, sin has its effects on our lives, and the lives of others right here and right now. God not only warns us about the consequences of sin, but He shows us examples of what happens when we do sin, He shows us the depth of its damage, He gives us a chance to learn the easy way!

David was a great king, a godly upright man, fearless leader, and is even described as *"a man after Gods own heart."* However, we all sin and fall short of the glory of God. Through David's sin, we see the depth of sin's consequences, but we can also learn from it. If you have never read 2 Samuel 11-12 you NEED to before you read any further. If you have read 2 Samuel 11-12 you NEED to read it again before you read any further! To make a long story short, David gives into his temptation and sins.

"It happened, late one afternoon, when David arose from his couch and was walking on the roof of the king's house, that he saw from the roof a woman bathing; and the woman was very beautiful. And David sent and inquired about the woman. And one said, 'Is not this Bathsheba, the daughter of Eliam, the wife of Uriah the Hittite?' So David sent messengers and took her, and she came to him, and he lay with her. (Now she had been purifying herself from her uncleanness.) Then she returned to her house. And the woman conceived, and she sent and told David, 'I am pregnant'" (2 Samuel 11:2-5).

The depth of the damage of sin did not end at ruining the heart of Bathsheba and dragging her into his lust. Bathsheba had a husband as well. Uriah was a courageous upright man who was out in battle. David was going to be in trouble if he did not do something to cover up his sin. His sin led to lying and deception. David sent to bring Uriah back home and spend time with his wife hoping that they would lay together, but Uriah being an upright man did not feel he deserved to be home when his fellow soldiers were out at war. Now how was David going to cover his tracks? The lying and deception did not work, so David resorted to murder.

"In the morning David wrote a letter to Joab and sent it by the hand of Uriah. In the letter he wrote, 'Set Uriah in the forefront of the hardest fighting, and then draw back from him, that he may be struck down, and die'" (2 Samuel 11:14-15).

Sin escalates rapidly. It went from David being lazy, to lust, to adultery, to lying, and then to murder. The sins that David committed had not only harmed him but also damaged the lives of many others. Those damaged were Bathsheba, Joab, servants, Uriah, and now a child! Unfortunately, the effects of sin did not end there. Even after David had repented, the child had died. Sin digs deep. The damage is great and will eventually lead to death!

James 1:15 says it like this, *"then desire when it has conceived gives birth to sin, and sin when it is fully grown brings forth death."*

Do we think about the depth of sin's damage before we sin? Do we think about the consequences when we lie to cover our tracks? Pray for God to keep you from sinning, so you do not have to experience the damage it can cause! Repent and pray for God to repair the damage that has already been caused!

NO EXCUSES

Ty Woznek | Lead Instructor of the Pastor's Academy

M icah says, *"He has told you, O man, what is good; and what does the Lord require of you but to do justice, and to love kindness, and to walk humbly with your God?"*

We Were Warned

In a Hebrew class, we were instructed to pick a verse and do an in-depth report on it. I loved the song growing up that quoted this verse. It was a sweet tune of a verse that is often a favorite of those who love Jesus. After studying it, I realize the tune missed the tone of what Micah was saying. Micah 6:8 was an indictment. God's people were to be punished, deserved to be punished, and they were without excuse. Why? God showed them the answer. They did not follow.

Hard of Hearing

Israel, like you and I, were hard of hearing. God showed them the way but they chose a different path. God showed them what good was, what justice was, love, kindness, and humility. These were rejected like at the beginning. Often when life is hard, we want to get mad at God, but the reality often is we ignored God. An older businessman said that if communication is the problem, it is that people are not listening, not that people are not talking. The bottom line is, are you and I listening to God?

Too Many Stories

When Doc asked me to write a couple of devotions on the devastation of sin as a storm of life, my heart sank. There are too many stories of heartache I could share. That is just starting with me. In all my years of ministry, they sadly add up. I noticed a common theme in many of the stories. They simply did not listen. Without fail, many pastors and I deal with an issue on Mondays that we addressed on Sunday, but the person was absent. I would not be surprised if some of you reading this today ignored what some of the pastors shared this past Sunday.

Hear

In Deuteronomy 6, Moses writes about loving the Lord our God with everything we have. He instructs us on teaching our children and talking about the Bible constantly. However, before that Moses wrote the bottom line, *"Hear of Israel, the Lord is God, the Lord is one."* There is more I could say on this, but here is what we need to do. Take a moment and simply ask God this question, "God, how well have I been hearing you?"

The Reality Is

We can be mad at God when he allows hard times in, but sometimes the reality is we knew the right answers but chose to go our own way instead. Micah 6:8 should be a depressing song. God gave them the answer; Israel did not listen. I guess that is why Paul so urgently warned us to no quench the Spirit. Like a good soldier, we would be better to answer "No excuses."

WE'RE MEAN, NOT GOD

Ty Woznek | Lead Instructor of the Pastor's Academy

People often reject the Old Testament because they view God as a mean grump. The fact check is quite the opposite. We were mean to God. We should be very careful to think we are better than God's people in the Old Testament. We do the same things. Evil is when we try to replace God with another god. Most storms in life are manmade whether by our own choices or suffering from the poor choices of others. As you read the rest of this, ask yourself if and how you are rejecting God. It is never too late.

God warned Adam and Eve not to eat the fruit of a certain tree. Adam and Eve rejected God's instruction. You and I suffer death, disease, and suffering as a result. God promised a Son that would redeem.

God warned Cain that sin wanted to control him. Cain rejected God's instruction and murdered his brother. Salvation seemed lost. God provided Seth.

God warned people to repent or he would flood the Earth. Mankind rejected God's instruction. According to creationist accounts, the world population was about six billion people. They all died. God saved Noah and his family.

God told Noah and his family to be fruitful and multiply and to fill the Earth. Instead, they congregated under one rule to make a name for themselves, rejecting God's instruction. God confused them by creating languages. God chose Abraham's family so the world would still know a way out.

God told Israel to go into the Promised Land that He provided for them. Israel sided with ten spies who said otherwise. A whole generation was wiped out for rejecting God's instruction. Only Joshua and Caleb were able to cross into the Promised Land.

God told Israel to destroy everything in Jericho. One man thought otherwise and brought failure to Israel and the loss of his family. God still forgave, and Israel took the land.

God told Israel to teach their children about who He is. Israel ignored God's instruction, and there arose in Israel a generation who did not know God. They suffered under tyranny from other nations. God provided Judges to redeem them.

God told Israel the Law, and their Elders were to lead them. Israel rejected God's instruction and requested a king like the other nations. The monarchy brought about the destruction of the nation. Through one king, David's line, God protected to bring us a Savior, Jesus.

God sent many prophets to warn Israel to repent and turn back to the Bible. They rejected and killed off God's prophets. God handed them over to their enemies. In all the promises of destruction, God also promised restoration and a Savior.

God sent Jesus to heal. Jesus was rejected and hung on a cross one time for all sin. God raised Him from the dead on the third day, providing the perfect way out of a nasty cycle.

Why does God love us even when we reject His Word repeatedly? God is a God of grace and mercy. The Old Testament should serve as a massive warning to us. God, is there something you are trying to tell me that I am rejecting?

4

STORM CHASER

Pastor Jayson Combs | Family Pastor

When I was in high school, the GREAT movie Twister came out (a little sarcasm). It was a movie all about being a storm chaser. It followed a group of meteorologists and scientists who, in an army of vehicles, searched for the biggest and baddest storms in tornado valley. What is crazy to me is that there are people who actually do this for a living. They chase tornados. They hope to get as close to one as they can.

For the past few weeks, we have talked about dealing with the storms of life. Hopefully, we have answered the nagging questions of why storms come into our lives and how to deal with them. For this week, however, let's change perspectives and talk about the storms in the lives of people around you.

I believe God calls us to be storm chasers. We are sometimes called to run head first into the storms of others so we can help them and love them. The beginning of the book of Nehemiah introduces us to Nehemiah, who was a man that was present and involved in the lives of others when storms hit.

Have you ever had a storm in your life and a person stepped into the middle of the storm to help you? _____

_____

_____

_____

How important was that to you? _____

_____

_____

_____

_____

Stepping into a storm in someone else's life is a pretty dangerous ordeal. For example, sometimes people do not want your help and/or sometimes you feel the storm is way over your head. Let's look to Nehemiah and his wisdom as he entered into a great storm to help his brothers and sisters in the decimated city of Jerusalem.

Nehemiah Chapter 1:

"Now it happened in the month of Chislev, in the twentieth year, as I was in Susa the citadel, 2 that Hanani, one of my brothers, came with certain men from Judah. And I asked them concerning the Jews who escaped, who had survived the exile, and concerning Jerusalem. 3 And they said to me, 'The remnant there in the province who had survived the exile is in great trouble and shame. The wall of Jerusalem is broken down, and its gates are destroyed by fire.'

4 As soon as I heard these words I sat down and wept and mourned for days, and I continued fasting and praying before the God of heaven. 5 And I said, 'O Lord God of heaven, the great and awesome God who keeps covenant and steadfast love with those who love him and keep his commandments, 6 let your ear be attentive and your eyes open, to hear the prayer of your servant that I now pray before you day and night for the people of Israel your servants, confessing the sins of the people of Israel, which we have sinned against you. Even I and my father's house have sinned. 7 We have acted very corruptly against you and have not kept the commandments, the statutes, and the rules that you commanded your servant Moses. 8 Remember the word that you commanded your servant Moses, saying, 'If you are unfaithful, I will scatter you among the peoples, 9 but if you return to me and keep my commandments and do them, though your outcasts are in the uttermost parts of heaven, from there I will gather them and bring them to the place that I have chosen, to make my name dwell there.' 10 They are your servants and your people, whom you have redeemed by your great power and by your strong hand. 11 O Lord, let your ear be attentive to the prayer of your servant, and to the prayer of your servants who delight to fear your name, and give success to your servant today, and grant him mercy in the sight of this man.'

Now I was cupbearer to the king."

Who is Nehemiah and where does he live? _____
_____
_____
_____

Who comes to Nehemiah and what is the great storm?
_____
_____
_____

Bible history question: Why were the walls of Jerusalem torn down, and why was the city in such bad shape? _____

_____

_____

_____

Three things Nehemiah did in the storm:

   1. He Had Compassion.

Reread verse 1 *("Now it happened in the month of Chislev, in the twentieth year, as I was in Susa the citadel")*. How did Nehemiah respond to the problem? _____

_____

_____

_____

What type of danger was Nehemiah putting himself in?

_____

_____

_____

Nehemiah's heart was broken for the people, 1 Peter 4:8-10 says, *"Above all, keep loving one another earnestly, since love covers a multitude of sins. Show hospitality to one another without grumbling. As each has received a gift, use it to serve one another, as good stewards of God's varied grace."*

Above all else, what does God tell us to do? _____

_____

_____

_____

In 1 Peter, how do we go about doing what God says?

_____

_____

_____

Do you sometimes find it hard to earnestly love people?

_____

_____

_____

What roadblocks stand in your way? _____

_____

_____

_____

2. He Earnestly Prayed.

Read Nehemiah's prayer in Chapter one. What specifically stuck out to you? _____

_____

_____

_____

Nehemiah begged God to save the people of Jerusalem. I Timothy 2:1-4 says, *"First of all, then, I urge that supplications, prayers, intercessions, and thanksgivings be made for all people, for kings and all who are in high positions, that we may lead a peaceful and quiet life, godly and dignified in every way. This is good, and it is pleasing in the sight of God our Savior, who desires all people to be saved and to come to the knowledge of the truth."*

How do these verses tell us to pray for people? _____

_____

_____

_____

   3. He Set Up Plans to Help.

Nehemiah 2:11-13: *"So I went to Jerusalem and was there three days. Then I arose in the night, I and a few men with me. And I told no one what my God had put into my heart to do for Jerusalem. There was no animal with me but the one on which I rode. I went out by night by the Valley Gate to the Dragon Spring and to the Dung Gate, and I inspected the walls of Jerusalem that were broken down and its gates that had been destroyed by fire."*

Nehemiah 2:17-18: *"Then I said to them, 'You see the trouble we are in, how Jerusalem lies in ruins with its gates burned. Come, let us build the wall of Jerusalem, that we may no longer suffer derision.' And I told them of the hand of my God that had been upon me for good, and also of the words that the king had spoken to me. And they said, 'Let us rise up and build.' So they strengthened their hands for the good work."*

What things did Nehemiah do to prepare the people to build the walls of Jerusalem? _____

_____

_____

_____

Read Colossians 4:5-6: *"Walk in wisdom toward outsiders, making the best use of the time. Let your speech always be gracious, seasoned with salt, so that you may know how you ought to answer each person."*

How does God tell us to prepare ourselves? _____
_____
_____
_____

What tools has the church provided to help you help people in their storms? _____
_____
_____
_____

ENDURING THE STORM

Jill Osmon | Assistant to the Lead Pastor

Enduring a storm is difficult; the kind of difficult that breaks men and women. Enduring a storm can seem impossible. Then God brings people into our lives; people, who try to help us endure storms, get through storms, and then thrive after the storm. Those people, the ones that speak into lives of people enduring a storm, that is whom I want to speak to for a bit today.

In the Bible, Job went through a pretty intense season in his life. He lost everything; I cannot imagine his pain and devastation that he endured. Job had a lot of friends surrounding him, with A LOT of opinions. Most giving some pretty terrible advice. His friends were going as far as telling him just to die because his life was so miserable. One friend had been sitting quietly, waiting, and listening to all that the others had to say, and he could not stay quiet any longer. His name was Elihu.

Elihu gave the perfect balance of love and truth; he did not allow Job to wallow in his circumstances, but he also gave Job solid advice. He goes on for a few chapters, and he has some difficult conversations with Job's friends and with Job. He did not diminish the storm Job was in, but he also stood firm in who God is. Job 37:14 says, *"Hear this, O Job; stop and consider the wondrous works of God."* We have to remember to point people to God during their storm. Self-help, self-esteem, self-whatever, does not help if they do not recognize that God is in control, and He is *"our refuge and strength, a very present help in trouble. Therefore we will not fear though the earth gives way, though the mountains be moved into the heart of the sea, though its waters roar and foam, though the mountains tremble at its swelling"* (Psalm 46:1-3). Elihu reminds Job who he is and Whom he belongs to. Although it seems simple, this simple fact brings a sense of peace and calm that only God can bring.

We will all have opportunities to help others through a storm and to endure a storm. We must be prepared to have some difficult conversations. The most important part of helping others through storms is to point them to God every single time.

GRATITUDE

Jill Osmon | Assistant to the Lead Pastor

Psalm 107:28-32 says, *"Then they cried to the Lord in their trouble, and he delivered them from their distress. He made the storm be still, and the waves of the sea were hushed. Then they were glad that the waters were quiet, and he brought them to their desired haven. Let them thank the Lord for his steadfast love, for his wondrous works to the children of man! Let them extol him in the congregation of the people, and praise him in the assembly of the elders."*

There are many conversations about how to get through the storm, how to endure it, but we do not usually talk about what we do after the storm. What happens when we survive? What does God expect of us on the other side? I know gratitude is the last thing that usually goes with a storm. Storms are devastating, they can destroy your life, and they can radically change your life. So how can we be grateful at the end?

Gratitude changes you. Think about it... when you are grateful your entire perspective changes. You see actions in a different light; you are more forgiving, more loving, and more Christ-like. However, gratitude is not a natural reaction for us; we have to strive for it. If we do not strive for gratefulness, we are useless. It says in Romans 1:21, *"For although they knew God, they did not honor him as God or give thanks to him, but they became futile in their thinking, and their foolish hearts were darkened."* An ungrateful heart is a heart open to bitterness, anger, worry, hate, and much more. When we go through a storm, we as humans can immediately become embittered because our perspective has been battered and abused. Gratefulness protects us. It allows us to gain a perspective that is focused on God and understanding that He is in control. It allows us to learn and teach from our storms.

God commands us to be grateful to protect us from our feeble human reactions. Be grateful, especially after a storm. Allow God to show us the what, the why, the deep down lessons that we need to learn through our storms. Gratitude allows that. It opens us up to being used by Him. Isn't that the most amazing thing to be done? To have our storms used to help others, to change us to be better ambassadors for Him.

Choose gratefulness!

EMPATHY

Donna Fox | Assistant to the Growth Pastor

I am fascinated by the movie "Twister." A group of storm chasers rushes after tornadoes in hopes of studying how they work and get a better idea of how to predict them in order to save lives. The idea of driving a vehicle quickly up one road and down another while trying to follow an unpredictable storm and facing risk of injury or death, well, it is quite exhilarating and gets the adrenaline flowing.

Sometimes in life, we are storm chasers. We run into the storm head on. More often, though, we are trying to run the other way, away from the storm. However, there is a lot to be learned from facing the trial, going through the trial, and coming out on the other side. We have that experience and can now empathize with others in the same or similar situation. I have had many life experiences that I can share with others in the same situation. They know I have been there, done that, and I truly know the pain they are feeling. There are many life experiences I have not experienced that others have. God makes us all unique. Just as the Bible tells us that we are each given different spiritual gifts, we are each given different life events to be able to comfort others. 1 Corinthians 12:26 says, *"If one member suffers, all suffer together."*

One of the great privileges of friendship is being able to help others through the storm. Sometimes it is sharing how we got through it, or how it changed us. Sometimes it is just listening and not talking. However, for them to know that you have experienced the same situation makes all the difference.

Have you experienced a storm? The loss of a baby? Financial difficulty? Addiction? The list goes on and on. How can you use your experience to help others? Is there a group at church you can mentor through? Is there a friend facing a similar problem that you can meet for coffee? God gave you this experience so you could help others. Just as Jesus suffered during his time on Earth, He was tortured, humiliated, alone, etc., He empathizes with us and knows how we feel in the same situation. He loves us and cares for us through our storm. Just as God comforts us, we need to comfort others around us and help them through their storm.

2 Corinthians 1: 3-4 says, *"Blessed be the God and Father of our Lord Jesus Christ, the Father of mercies and God of all comfort, who comforts us in all our affliction, so that we may be able to comfort those who are in any affliction, with the comfort with which we ourselves are comforted by God."*

LEAN ON ME

Donna Fox | Assistant to the Growth Pastor

Y ou have faced the storm. You have gone into the storm. You have come out of the storm. You survived! You are stronger because of it. Maybe you are not physically stronger, but spiritually stronger. Now what? How can you use your experience for God's glory?

If you have lost a loved one, join a GriefShare group. We have a great group that meets every Wednesday night. Sharing your story of survival and how you coped may be just the story someone needs to hear. If you have suffered addiction, or come from a family touched by it, check out The Road. This group meets every Tuesday night and is always looking for people who can empathize with their situations. Did you go through a cancer scare? So are many others around us. Reach out and offer to talk (or rather listen!) as they may just need someone to talk to today that has been through it and understands.

How can you help someone in need? First, take them to Scripture. They may not be strong enough to open the Bible and find the right verses of comfort, but you have been there, you know what might help. Write it down on a 3 x 5 card so they can find it easily and read it repeatedly. Next, pray for them. 1 Thessalonians 5:17 says, *"Pray without ceasing."* Intercessory prayer is very powerful. Another thing you could do is to send a card or text of encouragement. Let them know you are available to talk anytime.

If we humble ourselves and put ourselves in others shoes, we begin to realize what they are feeling and how sharing our experiences might help them through it. In 1 Peter 3:8, Peter writes to Christians, *"Finally, all of you, have unity of mind, sympathy, brotherly love, a tender heart, and a humble mind."* Paul also encourages empathy in Romans 12:15, *"Rejoice with those who rejoice, weep with those who weep."*

It has been said: You are either going into a storm, you are in a storm, or you have just come out of a storm. In any case, it is God's plan, and God will carry you through it. He wants you to learn from it and grow from it. When you reach out to another going through a similar situation, you will bless them. Who knows, sometimes it is the other way around and YOU are the one who receives the blessing! Reach out today.

BE A LIGHT

Jen Combs | Wife of Lead Pastor Josh Combs

I am currently sitting on a plane heading toward Orlando. Have you ever taken a flight to Orlando? It is full of families with little kids that are screaming. (I can say this because I normally am that family!) Not to mention I am squished in a seat that is too small with my husband next to me who is a little too excited, listening to his rock music pretending that I am his drum set. Did I mention that I am working on five hours of sleep? To top it off they stuck us in an exit row. Not the exit row with extra legroom either. It is the one that has less leg room and does not recline.

The truth is we all faces storms in our lives. They may not all be as little or insignificant as traveling woes, but we all face them. Sometimes they are thunderstorms that just leave a little bit of damage or ruffled feathers. Sometimes they are tornadoes that wreak havoc and destruction in our lives that take years to rebuild. The question is what do we do when we are in them? How do we cope? Let's look at God's Word and see what He has to say. Go to Philippians 1:12-14. Paul was writing this letter to the Philippian church while he was in prison for preaching the Gospel. I would say that is quite a storm, at least it would be for me. Paul says, *"I want you to know brothers, that what has happened to me really served to advance the gospel, so that it has become known throughout the whole imperial guard and to all the rest that my imprisonment is for Christ. And most of the brothers, having become confident in the Lord by my imprisonment, are much more bold to speak the word without fear."*

Paul continued to love and honor Christ, even through his storm. He did not decide that because it was so difficult not to follow Christ. So often, we as Christians encounter difficulty, and we flee the things of Christ thinking this could not possibly be from God. We lose our brains and revert to our old ways. During his trial, people saw Jesus in him, and he in turn directed them to Jesus. Through Paul's actions, other people came to know Christ and others were strengthened in their relationship. People are watching you...always. Your unsaved spouse is watching you, your kids, neighbors, extended family, and people at your job. They are watching to see how you deal with difficulties. Are you doing right? Difficulty is not an excuse to sin and do wrong. Always do right. How are you talking during your difficulty? Are you bringing your conversation back to Jesus? Are you whining, complaining, and cursing God? Are you looking for what God is trying to teach you in your storm? Are you so bitter you cannot see through the clouds? Remember, people are watching you, so be a light for Him. Glorify God in your storm.

WHY?

Jen Combs | Wife of Lead Pastor Josh Combs

T his past May, Josh and I were able to go to Florida and serve with an organization that works with families that have terminally ill children. One thing that struck me while I was there was this storm had no regard of people. There were rich people decked out in their matching family printed shirts raising awareness for whatever illness their child had. There were back woods country people with hardly any teeth. There were British folks. Mennonites dressed in their overalls and dresses. There were Mexicans and Arabs. One family that stuck out the most to me was a handsome, tall, athletic, African American man with his little boy. Even this big strong man could not fight this battle for his son. All types of people standing in line waiting for me to serve them dinner. It was only through Jesus that I could compose my emotions. I so badly wish I could tell them why. Why would God do this? Why would He let this happen? My heart broke as I stared into the eyes of these parents, siblings, grandmas, and grandpas who were going to be left behind without their little one. Maybe you are going through a storm that you are asking God "why?" I am going to tell you; I do not know. Just as in my head, I was telling these families. However, during unexplainable and torturous storms, we have to rely on God and His Word because that is all we have.

There is a story in the Old Testament about a man named Job. Job saw all kinds of tragedy. He was struck with illness, lost his fortune, and even all of his children. His friends told him to turn from God. His wife told him to curse God and die. (It is a long book but worth the read if you are up for it.) Job stays faithful to God and at the end of his life, God restores. Job 42:12 says, ***"And the Lord blessed the later days of Job more than his beginning."*** He had more children and was richer than before. The Bible says, *"... And Job died an old man and full of days."* What do we learn from Job? To stay faithful to God through our storms no matter how awful they are and somehow on the other side of it, we are better than before. I do not know how that happens. However, God says in Isaiah 55:8, *"For my thoughts are not your thoughts, neither are your ways my ways, declares the Lord. For the heavens are higher than the Earth. So are my ways higher than your ways and my thoughts than your thoughts."* We have to trust in Him that He knows what is best even if it hurts or does not make sense. Remember God has felt everything that we feel. He has felt hurt, anger, betrayal, poverty, sadness, and hunger. He even experienced the death of His Son. In the midst of our storms, remember He loves us, knows what is best for us, and has felt everything we feel.

Psalm 34:18, *"The Lord is close to the brokenhearted."*

OUR MISSION

Matthew 28:19-20: *"Go therefore and make disciples of all nations, baptizing them in the name of the Father and of the Son and of the Holy Spirit, teaching them to observe all that I have commanded you. And behold, I am with you always, to the end of the age."*

REACH

At The River Church, you will often hear the phrase, "we don't go to church, we are the Church." We believe that as God's people, our primary purpose and goal is to go out and make disciples of Jesus Christ. We encourage you to reach the world in your local communities.

GATHER

Weekend Gatherings at The River Church are all about Jesus, through singing, giving, serving, baptizing, taking the Lord's Supper, and participating in messages that are all about Jesus and bringing glory to Him. We know that when followers of Christ gather together in unity, it's not only a refresher it's bringing life-change.

GROW

Our Growth Communities are designed to mirror the early church in Acts as having "all things in common." They are smaller collections of believers who spend time together studying the word, knowing and caring for one another relationally, and learning to increase their commitment to Christ by holding one another accountable.

The River Church
8393 E. Holly Rd. Holly, MI 48442
theriverchurch.cc • info@theriverchurch.cc

BOOKS BY THE RIVER CHURCH

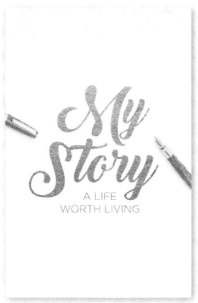

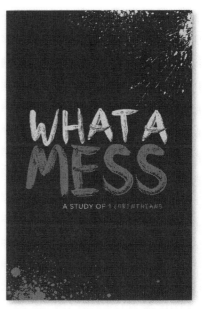

Made in the USA
Charleston, SC
28 September 2016